CW00820000

OUT FOR AIR

Olly Todd lives in East Sussex with his girlfriend and their daughter. His poems have appeared in *Ambit*, *The Rialto*, *Vice*, *Prototype*, *Five Dials* and the *Clinic* anthologies. His pamphlet, *Odeum Spotlights* (Rough Trade Books, 2018), was long-listed for the Michael Marks Awards.

ALSO BY OLLY TODD

Odeum Spotlights (Rough Trade Books, 2018)

Out for Air

OLLY TODD

Penned in the Margins

LONDON

PUBLISHED BY PENNED IN THE MARGINS
Toynbee Studios, 28 Commercial Street, London E1 6AB
www.pennedinthemargins.co.uk

First published 2022

Printed in the United Kingdom by TJ Books Ltd

ISBN
978-1-913850-07-4

CONTENTS

The Fuel	11
Tides	14
Leaving Goshen	15
The Spiralist	18
Yes, Oleaginous	19
Walking to Camberwell	21
NX RD	22
Ether Including Voices	24
Oaks	25
Low Tops	27
Ululation	29
Features of a Flight Path	31
Century Boulevard	33
Marines	35
Repose on the Flight into Egypt	37
Is This to Be That	38
Now	39
Sparrow	41
Rocks	43
The Room of a Mile	50
The Aircraft in the Space Below the Plane	52

Two Thoughts on a Hartlepool Sound Mirror   54

The Replacement   56

Tilia   58

Memories of a Sponge   60

TIXE   62

Milan   64

Just Think   65

O'Meally Frees a Seagull   66

Arisings   69

Cool   71

Us and Them   74

Entonox   77

Yan, tyan, tethera

Out for Air

The Fuel

A man so Embarcadero as to be emanating bridges.
The big red one.
The one over the oil farms.
Any but the one that rippled.

For one skater in the backseat of his future
to travel safely across.
For another fishing out a windcheater in the rucksack
of his ambition
to shelter under.

And the bridges are endless
beyond the cantilever
of reality
and the waters are friendly, lapping
at the trusses

and Cow Hollow High's canteen chairs
look between their legs
for his manoeuvres; its scholars

grip their pens;
its corridor floors shine.

A man so Presidio as to be the plateau of hills.
The eight-hairpin cobbled one.
The one with the hotels with the cellophaned bear claws
    for breakfast.
The one mellowing out past west-flank Black Rock.
Any but the one where speeding car
wing mirrors brush
T-shirt sleeves.

For one skater timing traffic from a hillcrest café
to get the green lights.
For another re-reascending
to roll instead of stroll for a welcome sec,
blissing out calves, quads, glutes.

And the hills are summitless
above the bedrock
and the gradients are kind, rendering
off the curbcuts

and the glass eye of prejudice cracks
on the mirror held up
by his graphics.

A man so Soma as to be the fuel of foundries.
The one where the baseball diamond now stands.
The pierside one.
The locomotive one shipping out
boxcars of fuss, any but
the one bringing them back.

For one skater to gain his stability, geometry, nimbleness
and another and another and others
and the sparks are innumerable that leap
from the fires
and the welds are honest, floating
on the bearings.

And the Ellesses
and the toast raised in polystyrene cups
and the humility in a twoscore of shout-outs
resound with my crew and I.

Tides

If that's the pavement rolling towards us
through the art department phone box like a tide,
it follows that the focus puller's glove
turns out to be lunar gravity.

The phone box is a man standing in the swash,
riveted together, filled with a conversation,
willing his abdicating collapse onto dry sand,
something like phone-in radio to cut out the one

sage-sounding chirrup in the dawn chorus,
the softly clicking clasps of makeup boxes.
If only we were as straight-backed and pomaded,
as sure about wine, as gastrically muscular

when pecking prosciutto-wrapped melon off a fork
or biting a ghost from the air above some stairs,
peddling a boat over fetched surf cradling
a rivet gun; strange for a tool eh?

Leaving Goshen

British Nuclear Fuel Limited
greenlights new Seascale reactor
claims the news. A computer
generated model tilts onscreen

through a crane shot
from an underwrought Isle of Man
over a repeated code of fretless waves,
a digital Irish Sea.

They've overlooked the railway line
that fastens sea to land like a brass zip here.
My mind's eye puts it in.
I'm fourteen.

A journey home is relived.
A bus and two trains from Bury
via Bolton and Barrow. It's evening
and I'm upping my personal

stereo's bass to phrase-match
the train's monochord beat and sirenise
the calls of the ancillary gulls and parson
my attendance at the altar

that is train window Solway sunset.
Of its colour scale there's nee swatch like.
The sky's boom is one only air over water
can have. I've spent the day padded up

skating vert alone
at a leisure centre named Goshen,
aptly I suppose, after all
it did have its treasure cities

of cultivated labour,
the twelve-foot vert ramp being Rameses;
the divisive new midi
with facing extensions was Pittim.

Both diagonally terrained
in chestnut masonite
consistent with surfacing's new wave.
The coping, unforgettably

chunky: a stretch to link
its ample diametre to irrigation ducts
on the Nile's blue Bubastis branch?
On the drive south that morning

we'd stopped at that services
known for its bridge café
connecting north and southbound sites.
'You'll get to know this road

like the back of your hand over the years
lad.' The M6 flashed by below
in high duty alloys, hot bonnets
glisking at nineties and tons.

The Spiralist

(Watson) has suggested the term 'spiralist' for the socially, economically and geographically mobile.

RONALD FRANKENBERG, *Communities in Britain*

Down the blacksmith's the gossip's he's one of those spiralists.
Concerned with the motorcars of visiting sociologists but no
    car of his own, just the wish.
Our oats spiral, broadcast for our lazy pigs.
The runes spiral, hard carved round our Saxon cross.
And the sun, well, it's yet again by Eskdale fell yet we move not.
Gosfer folk is Gosfer folk, that sun now nigh Hardknott.

Fell farmers come down for darts, may bout their boys with
    lowland hands, yet mix they do not.
The yellow insides of a scorpion, torn peaches, could
    Harrison's new 'dozer combine them?
Egremont for a matinee, the Bull for a drink, his Bristolian
    sleeplessness welcome at song.
We'll fetch him a Sunday shirt from Whitehaven.
Then he'll be gone.

Yes, Oleaginous

A new part of town, a new coffee shop.
You may have switched your work route,
begun a new job, or you're hotdesking
at some pingpong-tabled shared work place
with food trucks outside

parked against the Victorian granite curb
stones of the wide tarmac pavement
whose darker, smoother middle strip
points the theorist to water
company budget fiddling.

Banh Mi & Son daily by nine already busy
ribbon-slicing carrots
ahead of the lunchtime rush for Hanoi chicken.

Stand upwind
if you don't want your clothes to smell.

It won't be long before you identify
one member of this coffee shop's morning shift
as an oleaginous whittret whose service,
every day from the queue,

you'll pray

to be spared. The film sleeves
of the neat rows of ham,
bacon and cheese croissants
quivering in the cabinet's heated air
like flyfishing lures or indeed the surface
of the silver water on which they glibly bob

appear

to be the only moving thing
in every commute you've ever taken.
Not even your eyes, blurring
with abeyance, go anywhere.

Walking to Camberwell

When crisis loans from intact pockets
swim back to the brewery drains
and droning night buses
that were their usher and combat,

bib up and be brandished
with a Venezuelan meat and rice plate
of seared plantain and hot red Tapatio
and five-pound margaritas in frosted

echoic plastic glasses;
chequered vinyl tablecloths;
an old ray telly armed above the till
showing soft focus Spanish soaps.

In the time since – time stretched
into posable periscopic closed circuitry
positioned over your shoulder –
at last: the work, the relocation, her womanliness.

NX RD

I

Dinner earlier at the team cantina Argentina
was good although the starters trumped the mains as per.
The Transworld article *Waterloo to Anywhere*
was a let down too, omitting, as it apparently did,
my tennis court grind. I beat furs and fold throws,
listen to the heartbreak guys, only one of whom is yet
to lace the boots that would better will his drowning.
Next I go for Bonnie's *Angel From Montgomery*,
fork old tuna from the ramekin.

II

I'm Stig, immer durstig, altruistic.
That Lennon song on mam's labour tape was true.
I'm still to wire the speakers from lounge to kitchen
like home but the Bluetooth carries well. Ah nightcap

city, rattley rocks. It had been a time to skid a mile
in life's-a-beach shoes; itch in Fresno denim; go Cajun;
load the jukebox, and circle the Marquis bar. New Cross
from the perspective where no student is ugly anymore,
not even the greenhairs who hit the loos in threes.

III

We loved it when that actor would smoke,
would smoke away wholesome America like a cist burial.
When he smokes and stamps his feet in the truckstop
snow having locked his lighter in the rattletrap cab
our cortisol lessens like we'd steadied the bore
through something deep and brittle. Pre-credit-crunch
Belgravia free-booze parties became those parties
in arena carparks where gamegoers chant and douse
in lime their tailgate-barbecue carne asada.

Ether Including Voices

Is the image of your children, your ballons en laine,
to whom you read Dahl including voices on the train, better
than family life? The picture strikes my head and sleeves
me in the drugget dividing us through the carriage.
I get greener and greener about its matter.
You close the book to field questions. The eldest asks the age
of his oldest granddad. The youngest asks can raisins be made
back into grapes. The train holds a collection of killables
beside you, and I, too hot in a blue coat, will stall in a charity shop
upon realising I've walked too far ahead, find
Dennis Potter's 'The Changing Forest', get distracted, go home,
cook, and forget about all this until now.
And now is ether. Atheist ether. Ether at work on freezer bees,
resuscitating bodywork; it's Reno, *Reno*, the brink, the exploso.

Oaks

Mister like you he had squandered a kind of child.
His was a river tearing into its meanders, blind to the desert
    ahead.

What was left to nurse, a gratis Tecate?
And mister it was hot. Not 1976 hot, but hot.

A couple of years thereafter and in the cooler spring he came
    along.
The town kestrel overhead.

Someone had assembled an exit sheet of directions via the
    cut-up technique.
Unlimited three-point turns like gaming rewards footnoted
    for dead ends and piers.

Your terroir: a stone keep in a circle of oaks, mines not
    monasteries, some lowish fells.

Grandeur, tankard-clanking vim, new learning: spectres in
the vodka windows all.

You were picturing sanctuaries on higher ground: the
Dolomitic Alps, Veneto, Ampezzo.

Here Hepburn, Hemingway, Havelock and Bond evaded
their demons for a while. Gunners on spikewheel bikes
in Bond's case.

Atmosphere: après-ski cheer, stoicism, dissimulation.

A certain Angelo Dibona gets kudos.
In ascending both the Dolomites and our own highest peaks,
in conquering what you hid from by surmounting what
hid you, he has tied up the story like a clove hitch.

Low Tops

Then, in another dream, the precociousness
of street skating's achievement
in today's money.
A two-year-old Guy in black Enigmas

freeing the impossible from freestyle.
Rudy at three in combats and a flannel
destroying flatground on Hollywood Blvd.
Gabriel cavemanning a fifteen-stair

a week or so before his fourth birthday.
And, at five, Paulo the elder fastplants
in cutdown Caballeros.
Foam like the cream fat of deep cuts

there between the Rat Bones decals
and Rip Grip that tamed the padding
the scissor job exposed.
A skate shoe industry built

on low tops beckoned,
a few years ahead in reality
but no less reliant on the innovations
of the young. *We boys face the world*

shoulder to shoulder these sons
write with art pens in gang letters
on the bus benches and handrails they skate,
leaving behind two messages, at least two.

Ululation

Joe

Unplayable in territories here
where broadcast formats alternate the line,
my DVD of *A Visual Sound*
abandoned back in two thousand and eight.

Toyota

Consigned to storage, rubbing shoulders with
the first print lookbook Palace ever did.
This morning though by chance technology
undid its shackles from those playback bonds.

Is there something I can help you with?

A mallrat on a board in Super 8
emerging from behind a parked school bus
mid-air down in the western avenues
where San Francisco gifts its skaters most.

Killer's Gun from S.F.

The kickflip up the curb at Wallenberg
lands on the beat of 'Barracuda Blue'.
The palindromic driveway footage cut
amid the green bench tricks at Union Square.

Blah blah ahhh

What's there to glean from reconciling this?
It's how my adolescence shaped itself.
The wet ink of the now that dried survives
the fingertips we use to trace its worth.

Features of a Flight Path

Outside, the swimmable Sunset Strip was timelapsing
into its nightly stilled flourish of bleeding tail lights.
In the Saddle Ranch you could hear
the mechanical bull's crunching gears and the howls
of its vulnerable riders
thrown doomed over their belts.
Punch bag hooks and eight ball breaks
gave grammar to the drunkenness and incurious sycophancy
catching up brings about.
We all laughed when Shimizu reminded us of the time
I got the FlyAway
from Union Station to LAX
simply to ask a question of my booking agent:
how much to change the date of my flight, or something.

The lass a was ga'an wid –
jewellery brand; sliding-doors garden apartment off Wiltshire;
prismatic blue jeep (Tonka truck writ large from Sport Billy's
     holdall);

Balboa Beach country club membership –
had mentioned Christmas with her folks in Phoenix and that
her mother had already stocked up on Jameson's and Newcastle.
I thought I wonder why Cali parlance
omits the Brown Ale as the blue bus
beat traffic in the carpool lane like a whale.
As the blue bus disappeared in La Cienaga's wet maw like a
      plankton cloud.

That I travelled an hour plus
on a hot day in a cramped bus
to ask a question a search engine
could have answered
in half a second
matters less than the pause
in the hands-as-heartbeat wings
of the Somerset bird that broke flock
near the window as I closed
the shutters this Saturday afternoon
with you coming in from the en suite
lost in the dark like the light of a torch.

Century Boulevard

PART I

In which Jim Morrison describes a hotel where I once also stayed

'Atlanta has the most amazing hotel you've ever seen. You walk in from the outside and it looks like any other large hotel. You get in and you look up. It goes up about twenty-seven floors and the interior is like a Spanish courtyard. Architecturally it's hollow so all the rooms face each other across this vast garden arena. And the elevators are like, kinda like Victorian rocketships, and they're glass and so you go up to the restaurant in the penthouse level and it's completely encased in glass and so you get this strange sensation rising up twenty seven floors in this glass elevator. Oh somebody jumped one time.'

PART II

In which I describe a hotel where Jim Morrison once also stayed

Where's your hotel? she says.
At the end of the Century Boulevard, I say.
Century Boulevard, bitch! she says
and we get in the car.
The boulevard is tree-lined and true.
We get in the hotel and we look up.
We ride the glass lift up and down.
Albinoni's Adagio in G minor is playing in there.
I see teammates leaving their rooms
on various mezzanine corridors
which all face each other across the vast space
the glass lift vertically hurtles through.
The beauty of the world, its estuary sunsets
and storms, are not visible. Its thriving
farms; its ferns' fossilized leaves;
its lightning-hit promontories;
its goddamn rainbows half circling barren trees;
its roseroot blooming on the Wastwater screes.
It's Sunday in the Bible Belt
and impossible to get a drink anywhere.

Marines

Do you remember that day outside
the Alameda loft when The United States
Marine Corps tried to enlist me? Perhaps
I'd swayed in the dusty wind denatured.

Remember the station wagon pulling up
and those two baby shoebills stepping out? Sabres
slung low on goldbuckled belts, thick-wristed,
pulled around by a circuitry of hamstrings

and money and green sport.
Get back on the gridlocked beltway lads.
I am not your burgess; Barrow in Furness
was my blooding.

Leave me to this silhouette of a gasholder
in this photo I found, to this *C90* mix, the atavistic
music of the glovebox of early adulthood.
But this is just talk, from the bolted down

chairs of doughnut shops to the bridges
crossing mere suggestions of rivers,
blown through a cheap harp in G.
Other drafters, with no drive

or initiative in place, no curbside counsels,
are out there too; there's someone outside
now playing army. You can hear their tongue
moving over the grenade pin in their teeth.

Repose on the Flight into Egypt

How lonely to be awed by people,
find them funny or sexy.
To find a person funny or sexy is absurd.
The nival cadenza, calocarpa, scarlet moss,
the only red life in their unending white landscape.
How can we be so impressed, as sparkling duly viewing these
or oystercatchers
or northern lights
that we should laugh at a person or let go?
Even naked and quizzical, at their best,
still there shouldn't be power possessed as to stun.
In odeum spotlights they are merely small.
In traffic they are just skin.
To be gone into by someone though,
rephrased in their laughter,
is to sit up hip to hip in the soul's odeon,
is to have a stranger's hand guide you gently clear in a club,
accepting profoundly their apology.

Is This to Be That

Is this to be that complex in reverse?
The pugilist's grip holds nothing but its own
callouses. A plectrum's worth would do, no more.
The need to overpower to preserve is ironic
and perverse. I'm looking at a mug-height,
mid-oxidised bust of Caesar, wood filler in fissures
on three out of six pedestal facades; a goldleaf
embossed matte matchbox of sweet pea seeds (for me
and the bees). You, some plagiarised lines
from an Eye of Providence manifesto (aprioristically
true, to you. Or is it the other one?); a fairy sighting
ambrotype; a couple of houseguests farewelled
at the cowbelled door, two saluted waves of exoneration
of the way you guys do things from the front path.

Now

The sea that tweaked the blue canoe,
the sea behind the wave,
strives and does not yield.

Is anything more exciting than cars parked in a field?
An air frost, a running steed, un nuovo ponte *in 2020*
built over the old one like a gantry crane?

Those hefty brown bricks hewn raw
you'll find from Cleator to Keekle, Settle to South Philly
and *only the other land parts!* of the entire Eastern Seaboard.

Now I'm left looking for the perfect piece
of dimpled concrete
to cut the corners of sculpting.

I'm writing standing up,
inverting the asteroid split
that clouds the open clouds.

It's the boy lambs cry,
libraries of lambs
falling from the falling-forward eaves.

Unsolder the circuit boards
of the alarms and Tannoys
at Carl's Junior in Malibu,

Pacific Coast Highway.
Dusty brown glass windows with brown steel frames in
    direct sunlight –
break the windows with something.

Sparrow

You could
liken today's heavily tattooed to
arsonists dozing through a
protest riot's halfbrick rain, only to
wake hotly like an impala or
clown and spring into action. The
seized opportunity of permission. A
freckled Salford grifter streetcast for a
Benetton youth campaign; a
Nunhead maybe or Peckham kebab shop, a
tanned shoulder, tongue wiggling her
blue wine, editing selfies of her
unruliest moment. Where are the
Crab Fair's young gurners? I think it was

winter 1956 that saw Edith Piaf regard as
Greek her Broadway notices, toss them at an
interpreter, and smile wide her
lipstick charade. Whether America did or did not

deserve her, having begged this

vogue repute to assert a

swell in the Big Apple, mercifully the doubt it

recycled would go on to rust on the wet meds that

swamped her auburn follicles. And the

last inclination of the urban century to

fetishise the rural West went with her

withered orange hair on the 10th of

October 1963.

Rocks

Night and day
it seems superbikes
blast living metal
past my window,
bringing to mind an old poet.
Sod it man, let's go
to New York and find him.

We'll start in Brooklyn
repainting launderette signs
in our imaginations

for spending money.
Yes let's us to fair Brooklyn fly
to fix those faded launderette signs
and let's us down in Breuklein find
the road to that undaunted mind.

On Greenpoint's squalid alley tiles
we'll rebulb broken launderette signs,
the letters and their loops admired
by gangsters on their stoops, retired,
keen to know the briar rose.

Then it's over Williamsburg Bridge,
the planet's most suspended skate,
a bridge to give our scheme its theme.

Through the side effects of urethane
we'll work out what's illegal,
what's to gain.
It would be fun if,
saving our dimes,
we flicked nickels
in the piano jar
at The Blue Ruin.

Funner if, pushing Harlem
streets, our wheels stop
in melted asphalt
to cabbies' chagrin.

And if, using a stripped pine limb,
we poke at this blacktop
and vent the poor islet.

No man is an islet
but one maniac
tears up this river-
long, rock-strong
land limb on a cock rocket.

Let's us have the sticky
road grab our wheels
before his bike, blocking him,
our target, his kickstand
slowly sinking, measuring
the depth to which
the Radio City-reflected sun
penetrates the street.

Down Manhattan's silky streets
we'll crawl the jewellers smartly gowned.
This feeling city's green man bleats
that Amsterdam is diamond town.

That there and only there
can certain stones be replaced.
Stolen, once-worn things.

This isn't Damstraat
east of Amstel
flexing its marshland muscle,
but a city
in a tired wonderland
built by a city
built by diamonds
looking for farce, regret,
the pencil that winds its cassette.

Haven't we called him?
Rifled him the odd
dawn yodel?
A souring ricochet
like the Dakota Building's
bullet ballet?

Did we call incessantly,
from Valentina Quay

to The Fish Gap?
Our hoarsest throat
soothed on succotash
spooned in behind
the immutable masks
of the day –
born-again, sonarman, beard.

The hare lies down on Broadway
before the young asp,
up from the sewer,
goes for its eyes, fizzing
out the fruitstall colours
that mix there
with the light of cars.

Hey little nightmares you,
get out of our head
so we may trace
his former daredevilry –

Ducati tyremarks
cornering Wall Street;

peyote buttons scattered
like breadcrumbs
through Battery Park;
yawning, gold-sequined
females pressing the wrong
buzzer on the brass
address plate
of his apartment block.

Let's us, debonair, refine
our choice of wine at the Carlyle.
By way of snare our table maps
a Bordeaux boulevard of traps.

Nothing, poet doesn't show.
Perhaps we should have snared a vole
to lure the fox Hughes made him know
who bleeds its stink across the snow.

So, back to our room
so smoothly; tarmac
rehardened, glassed
by the cool night.

On the TV a newsreader relays
first there came the soakaways –
a geological concern,
invisible until it turns
deserts inside out;
a diner was swallowed
by a sinkhole.

Unnerving, the resultant
rocks in the kitchen:
boulders becoming stairs
that no one lived to climb.

The Room of a Mile

Look who the hell it is I got in the back of my old Civic right now.
It's a three-door so I'd had to sidestep in.
And now the Bowery buildings are doing limbos
of their own to look down their chins at the goings on.
Some of them flesh-and-rib skyscrapers don't forget
so as they move for vantage
looking like grass in the wind the sunlight
on the worn beige upholstery
is variably manifest and veiled.
Yesterday had been art: the room of a mile of pipe in segments
and a mile of dirt in rows
and the tone poem librettos
in glass cases at the MOMA.
Today the plan is creole chicken wings, beers, darts…
Skating? Not if we toss that thing in the East River first!
Well-rehearsed for days like these
why I brought a board beats me.
Half the afternoon we spend finding a suitable skateshop
at which to stash it overnight while a not insubstantial part

of the rest of the trip is given to making arrangements
for its collection, navigating Sundays, public holidays,
rainstorms the government texts you about.

The Aircraft in the Space Below the Plane

The aircraft in the space below the plane
moved like slow lasers. For lasers at least
this was slow. For anything else it was faster
than anything. Tracing avenues they moved
like roaches beelining the wire of a tipped cage.

Above Piccadilly's blanktape marketing –
iron poured molten over perry pears and yuccas –
the aircraft moved like slow black lasers.
At least for lasers this was slow and black.
For anything else it was faster
and whiter than anything.

Once – ich war zweimal über Hamburg –
it was the opencast mines and quarries in clouds
that struck me in the space below planes.

Today, the helicopters and light craft
between me and the West End have swept left
from the Chilterns, right from the Downs,
rattling chassis seams and entering
the lottery of high ascent.

They moved like slow, black perforated lasers.
This was at least for lasers slow, black and perforated.
For anything else it was faster,
whiter and more whole than anything.

Two Thoughts on a Hartlepool Sound Mirror

Floods on good brunches (brie
and grapes, warm baguette, a bistro
in Hove – cerebellum-buttressing stuff);
vast ingress tubing our summer rides

on the Ferrocarill de Soller or La'al Ratty;
inundations turning date nights to geos…
Thank you Palo Alto's agilest minds
for the numbers in ineluctable red circles

climbing in the corner of the screen.
Were it at all audible would the onrush
have stirred a dormant MOD sound mirror
for fair early warning? Those pre-radar

defenses, brutalist bowls upended,
since gone to seed, sprouting rebar – sonic
marshmallows of Hartlepool, Romney Marsh.
Mallorca; mountain roads,

a preclusive hand, a seething eye turned
from the coach window denying the ravine
below is there. Something reflecting
far off sound, getting closer, zip shape,

fecund, guiding the unstable substrate,
bringing word the new gen set to
denounce social media are twinkles
in their great grandas' eyes as prophesised.

The Replacement

De nacht roept
NTL NEDERLAND

I

We are in hysterics over the size
of Southend Airport. Looking back,
what cynics. Don't the circles we insist
on travelling 'tessellate in hell' as well?

Phones already off, we get an idea
of the time from our bureau de change receipt,
walk the matter of metres
to our departure gate, animos solito.

Memory flows
Cool round the bone
NORMAN NICHOLSON

II

The jewellers is found in the rain.
The new neighbourhood is navigated
on the half-hexagonal Prinsengracht. Of the arts
it is learned cinema is youngest and sees life deepest.

Cyclists are looked out for from the pavement
in the improving weather. While the thaw is not inevitable,
summer is not a myth, Haarlem, is not a myth, Breuklein…
the arguments of your thousand bijou attics

sliding off each other like essays in plastic wallets.
Below the hook that would have winched pianos, grain,
the grudge match of the gable room is sung
by the slow lung of its winestained billowing curtain.

Tilia

Cumbersome in the street lime,
wood pigeons, back again.
A family out for air, dad in tow,
a weekday. Crunch time. Claws

of rain on the window. An arsenal
of tennis balls, Aerobies, Lucozade
appears wired to them but in the consoling
manner of biodegradability.

Dad does shorts with a City Boy watchcoat.
Mum, deprecating, Di-ish
uplook, strawweight body a headrace
for the millwheel water

of their lives, worries her facemask
at the corner by the daily briefing graph
of a malerected bamboo fence fringing
a terracotta garden wall.

Certain shoots – fall
Metrics – telegraphing axis: Pavement
Desiccation Rate. Apparently some guys
just got to skate, heedlessly

cramming Daubeney Fields,
rightly dubbed 'Cummins Bumps'
now of course. We're out of spirit
vinegar for the limescale in the loo.

The comb handle won't do.
The lemonyellow comb,
free in some Qantas Air or Ozen
Beach resort welcome pack

years ago. A work trip would be so
holy now. What else… needle
and thread, toothbrush and paste,
single blade razor, eye mask.

Memories of a Sponge

No ordinary shower gel; aphrodisiac
shower gel. I get the abstrusity.
It lavas through white knuckles.
The one small black plastic bottle of it there was

running out concurrently with the summer
affair it sustained; afternoons julienned
into cigarettes, cider trips, showers, repeat
by the knives of this, one's latest inter-fling timeout.

The itemised acts never allowed to blot or cultivate.
Ephesian imperatives came loudly and empty-eyed
from a driverside window on the Bull Ring.
Hardly a milligram of nostalgia

other than the flippantly memorable,
this too is about as rose-tinted as dentist's water
and as neutral, as swill-worthy.
Years later, an inquiry at a branch of its maker

left of the lonely south exit at Waterloo
known only by locals, smokers, inductees
to the Palace Waywards Boys' Choir; all three…
discontinued, sometimes pops up on eBay.

TIXE

Walking beneath an exit sign and looking back,
the neon word reads backwards.
Is this where we're at, this lack
of an overlapping world?
No more feathered birds, slated roofs?

The hands of the matchday huddle repel
like science bench magnets?
We are in a brightly lit restaurant at midnight
when the above separates,
when the abutted separates

and forces the understanding of a life
that is totally possible to lead
intermittently in two dimensions.
We get the lamb chops and ice tea
and say the overlapping world was fine as it was.

This world-pair is too defined and readable.
For instance the pier above the beach where the race takes place
is today a mere hovering platform
with nothing by way of sides
giving those taking part in life no choice

but to jump. However tomorrow
or even later tonight the pier above the beach
is walled and tyre-hung with eyeleted rope.
You can still jump if you want
but you can climb now too.

Milan

I went away,
drank salted coffee.

Restrained a wild friend
with a café serviette.

Commissioned a cyanotype
of anma clouds in a prism.

Fed love
with policied silence.

Used your beautiful face
to ply oxytocin each night

in my choice of bunk.
Its material base

soon there for the latent
veer, the turn

back towards myself,
to you.

Just Think

The borrowed farmhouse by the sea, just think.
And something *Exile* on the turntable.

Love tension joining in the air the air
the ziplocked chicken carcass has released,

engulfing now the basil plant that a)
makes pity part of photosynthesis

and b) tastes more of Pernod than itself.
So let's relinquish all conjunctions then?

And lose 'of'? When the ice cream's this plain, well,
sphericity of scoop is balm, believe,

to fiscal aches established in a time
when Zippos made great gifts engraved or not.

Still foundering on rocks (read collar bones),

the sinking conversation perseveres

on blind autoausterity; veneers
intransigent and onside all at once;

what birds who fly with baskets in their beak
portend for us, a blind date through a friend.

O'Meally Frees a Seagull

Up in the gods at the matinee.
Onstage an affair, mostly astringent, false
starts in a rotating barroom inferable
through its stools and dregsy beer bottles.

With no interval scheduled
the upper circle takes on the heat
and hirsute textures of a greenhouse.
In this tropical air we nod at the stairs.

Afternoon tea at Fortnum & Mason
belies our deception: little deco tea tools
and a window over sunny Jermyn Street's
hand-visored work leavers.

In asking the waitress about pasteurised cream
it's necessary to tell a stranger about the bump
before telling your friends. Scones with butter
and jam it is then. Betrayal on the side.

Later at a Mayfair gallery, going along the line
of Blondey's blowtorched toast art
with Lucien outside stopping traffic
posing next to a black cab wrapped in his ad.

Twin superyachts breaching skate's anchorage
picking up fair winds in these postdiscretion age seas.
The best betrayal that day swoops into the azure air
of Monaco on O'Meally's Instagram.

He'd found a great lost gull on his hotel terrace and –
with a wiry white wing in each of his big Aussie hands,
indeed with the verónica pass of a matador –
flung it over the guardrail to freedom.

Keeping the sword of this wit obscured by the muleta
was a how-to-feint one-o-one and what we love most
about the footage are the gulls the freed gull joins
already circling between the tall buildings below.

Arisings

Gems and shrew bones forked from ground
turned over for something merely poetic
or decorative; sunset sillion or a rockery.
The quilted protest of the earth,
the dry whirlpool of it; careful, scarred ankle
ligaments, connately vulnerable Achilles tendons.
No quarry then; arisings,

diamonds delivered as coal,
charcoal delivered as a sapling bough.
Knots push their way from wood eventually.
While on the gun we trust our feet will push us
from the blocks so we can once again run west.
Who could have guessed
the West Coast's first grey road would wind

to a Food & Wine already there?
It called for neon, incentivised
the valley's lack of light;

adventures fuelled by the newsstand, by wheatgrass.
Even the indifferent would ratch for a nail
to scratch into the bright window their verdict:
the myopia-ruined hawk trail, or elan

and the sedatives were the cause.
Promptly alive in – coming perhaps a century later –
convertibles, tour vans, bay vista hotels,
remember to escape
the spotlight in the foyer.
Faces brighten then drop with the memory
of the taste of catarrh.

Cool

I was on about the bus
whose cool seats held
all my things
and money.

Why did seeing where
on the sun they'd dug
the mine make getting
off seem innoxious?

The knowledge
of when to duck when
its stardom ends
in smithereens.

Nothing deschedules
these buses anymore
so it sped away
as is its wont

down a high street
very much like those
infinite ones. I chased
and I passed –

stammering to officials
where's the depot –
the shopwindow
lifestyle cash

can still buy you:
Holyrood House tea towels;
longburning sepulchre
prayer candles;

cocoa halva; greens
and white onions deigning
to the carcinogens
of treacling ham skin.

The street was crowded;
the warrant of June.
The '90s yellow brick
flats – shared lounges

perfect for the soap
omnibuses. That's when
things started to idle.
Laminate-floored

shells of clutter
and passiveness
couched as utilitarian.
Plastic floor lamps.

Nowhere for the ironing board.
Garish, thin spaces.
I can't drop the thought,
rapacious mind:

we must think out, up –
which clouds are above
you now? In what state
will I have seen them

if at all? Passing
the piercing moon,
letting slip the true
atrophy of their depth.

Us and Them

Unite the lucky.
Commission their oaths.
Leave bathtubs beneath chandeliers
untouched by champagne.
Consider filling them with champagne though.
Consider quarter-filling them with ash
but stump your rollies in the sand box at Southbank.
Hear the music you play
to boost your friends blow away on the wind.
Heatscreen Perrier bottles in fading degrees
to mirrors with photos of Marlboros and the Pogues.
Steal from the Burberry to give to the Prada.

Unite the rich.
Commission their oaths.
Don't flinch when wealth appears from the heavens.
Don't flinch when twenty-pound notes
float onto your upturned palms.
Commandeer the hotel rooms of the deserving,

the northern and the danced-out.
Hang stolen lingerie from the cistern
and give it drunkenly to your girl on her return
to the bedroom, modelling the oversized red two piece.
In the morning give the lobby staff the slip
and run when your ring tone alerts them.

Unite the young.
Commission their oaths.
Tremble at their sides from knowing
in the alley by the railway station.
Tell them the show wouldn't exist without them.
Tell them actually it would exist but would be terribly boring,
just you looking at yourself in the mirror all night.
Ride your T100 Bonneville, left wrist on your lap,
fingers drumming the benchseat,
head in an openface Bitwell helmet, gunmetal,
scanning Porto di Venezia east and west
for your Broom Scorpio speedboat, wood panelled.

Unite the brave.
Commission their oaths.
Collars-up, lean against the wall and smoke.

Collars-up, lean against the wall, prop one foot
and broodily exhale silver smoke.
See your boat in the cruise port and go,
Raising the anchor in your mind.

Unite the beautiful.
Commission their oaths.
Hug them and welcome your sweaty friends.
The heat in here is turning everyone red
and the guy in green threw up his crab & cranberry canapés.
Their sweet aversion to makeup and insistence
on popstud bottoms that collect rainwater, flare and bobble
only confounds one because where they go they glow,
even in this heat.
Deftly it is their midriffs that decorate.
Don't dream of asking them to host.
Don't dream of asking them to reabsorb the condensation
their sweat deposits on the sash windows
and heatscreened mirrors that adorn these walls.

Entonox

It felt like we'd have slipped right off Archway Road
despite only a plum roll gradient and millimetric scuff
of rain, such was our shared vertigo,
vetoed from triage for not contracting enough,
walking past A&E with its OD frontier,
cannula puppets still bidding they smoke,
no attrition for our cupidinous fear
or the soles of our shoes, not the merest stroke
of friction. The overfull bus stop bin;
the unresponsive taxi app; the four-a.m. chill;
the fresh sounds of other women
straining for established labour's Sangreal;
the lucky, strangled devils who reached theirs well
that night; the U-turning taxi with the road to itself.